Sleep

Claire Llewellyn

Explorer Challenge

Find out why bats
sleep upside down ...

OXFORD
UNIVERSITY PRESS

Contents

Going to Sleep

What happens when we need to sleep? Most of us go to a dark, quiet place. We lie down and our bodies relax. Our eyelids grow heavy and close. The world around us seems to disappear. We are asleep.

We might sleep in a bed, a hammock or on a mat; in a big city or outside under the stars. Whoever we are and wherever we live, humans and animals, we all need sleep.

We spend one third of our lives asleep.
That's about 122 days every year.

How about you?

Where do you sleep?

The Pattern of the Day

For most of us, our days follow a regular pattern. We wake in the morning when the sky is light. We might work or study during the day. We eat together, see our friends and often do something active. In the evening, as the sky darkens, we begin to get tired. We sleep in the night and wake in the morning, ready for a new day.

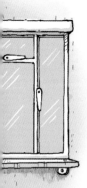

Did you know?

Doctors, cleaners, police officers, taxi drivers and many other people often have to work at night. They sleep during the day.

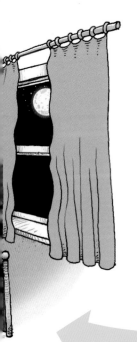

How about you?

What time do you get up?
When do you go to bed?

While We Sleep

While we sleep our muscles relax and our heartbeat and breathing slow down. However, our brain is hard at work.

Scientists aren't sure exactly what the brain does when we are asleep. They think it sorts and stores the new things we have learned during the day. The brain also checks the body. It makes sure the body has the right **chemicals** to grow, heal and fight **disease**.

Mum started her new job today.

... we store memories

How about you?

What new things have you learned today?

I had eggs for breakfast.

I performed in the school play.

$4 \times 5 = 20$
and
$20 \div 5 = 4$

... we sort the new things we have learned.

I can use the inside of my foot to kick a ball.

When we are asleep ...

... we forget things that aren't important.

My teacher was wearing a red jumper.

Dreams

When we sleep we often dream. Scientists aren't sure why. Some scientists think dreams help us to understand events that happened during the day.

Sometimes we have bad dreams and wake feeling worried or scared. But dreams aren't real and they can't harm us. When you go back to sleep you might have a nicer dream!

How about you?

Dreams can be very strange. Can you remember a strange dream you had?

How Much Sleep?

We all need to sleep, but there are no rules about exactly how much sleep each person needs. When we are young, we need a lot of sleep but as we get older we sleep less. In certain parts of the world, people **nap** during the day. Young children and elderly people often nap too.

There are 24 hours in a day. How many hours do people spend asleep? It usually depends on their age.

Age 0–3 months

14–18 hours

Age 4–11 months

12–15 hours (with naps)

Age 1–2 years

11–14 hours (with nap)

Age 3–5 years

10–12 hours

Age 5–12 years

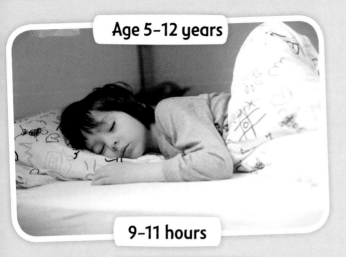

9–11 hours

Did you know?

Some workplaces have special rooms where workers can take a quick nap when they are feeling tired.

Age 12–18 years

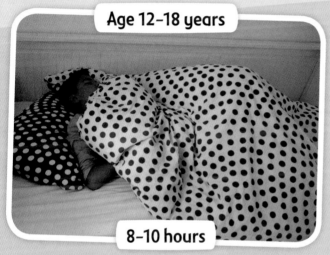

8–10 hours

Age 18–65 years

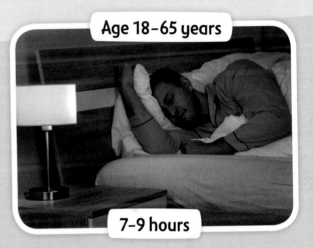

7–9 hours

Age 65+ years

7–8 hours (with nap)

How about you?

How many hours do you sleep?

13

Short of Sleep

Sleep is important to our health.
It affects the way we feel and behave.
Sleeplessness can affect us badly.

We are clumsier.

We have less energy.

How about you?

How do you feel after a
bad night's sleep?

We find it hard to concentrate.

Did you know?

There is no world record for going without sleep. Record books won't include one because a lack of sleep is harmful.

We make more mistakes.

We can't remember things as well.

We are grumpy.

A long time with no sleep can badly affect people's health. They can struggle to think clearly and they may see things that aren't really there – a bit like dreaming when they are awake!

A Good Night's Sleep

Try following these tips for a good night's sleep:

Relax before bed.

Go to bed and get up at the same time every day.

Make your bedroom cool and dark.

Exercise daily for at least 30 minutes.

Did you know?

Any artificial light can keep us awake, but computer, phone and TV screens give out a stronger, bluer light that can stop us falling asleep.

Avoid using a TV, computer or mobile phone for two hours before bedtime.

How about you?

What do you do before bedtime?

Animals and Sleep

Just like humans, animals need to sleep. They sleep at different times of the day and night.

Some animals sleep at night and are active during the day.

Some animals sleep during the day and are active at night.

Some animals are active at dawn and dusk. They nap both day and night.

Did you know?

Most birds are active by day. They find their food by sight, and need light to see.

19

How Much Do Animals Sleep?

Some animals need a lot of sleep while others need much less.

Tigers are carnivores and hunt large prey. After eating a big meaty meal, they enjoy a good long sleep. Tigers are powerful animals and don't have to watch out for **predators**.

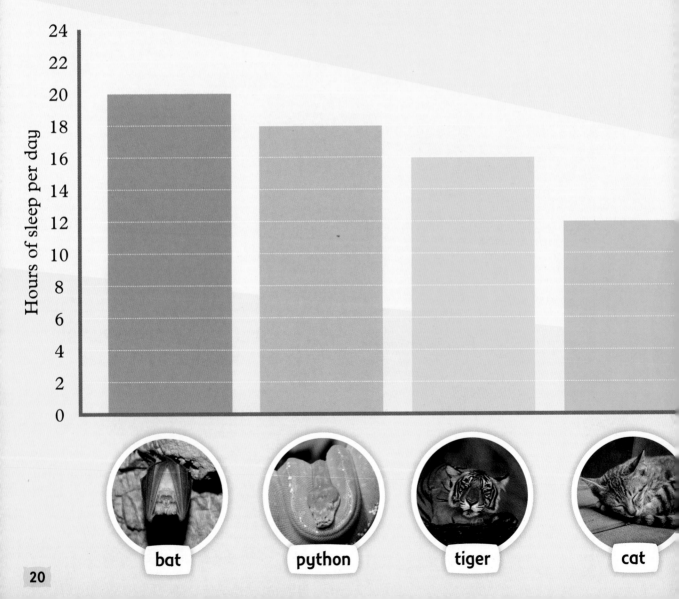

bat   python   tiger   cat

Horses and giraffes eat plants. They must feed for many hours to get the food they need. They also have to watch out for predators. These animals do not sleep much. They nap now and then.

chimpanzee

seal

horse

giraffe

Where Do Animals Sleep?

Many animals are careful about where they sleep. They need protection from danger and the weather.

This armadillo is sleeping in its **burrow**.

This bird is **roosting** in a tree.

Horses sleep in the open. They nap standing up.

Leopards dangle over the branch of a tree.

Many bats sleep in caves. They hang upside down. This helps them to take off when they need to fly. They can drop into flight.

Did you know?

Flamingos sleep in water. They balance on one leg. Some scientists think they do this to keep one leg warm and dry!

Half Asleep

Some animals do something really amazing: they sleep with one eye open and half their brain awake!

Most sea creatures don't breathe air as they get the oxygen they need from the water. Dolphins are different – they breathe air at the surface of the sea. By sleeping with half their brain awake, they avoid sinking and drowning.

Ducks and geese roost in flocks. Birds on the inside of the flock close their eyes and sleep. Birds on the outside of the flock keep one eye open for predators and one side of their brain awake.

Did you know?

In humans and many animals, each eye is controlled by the opposite side of the brain.

A Winter Sleep

Some animals spend the winter in a deep sleep called **hibernation**. Where these animals live, food and water are hard to find at that time of year.

dormouse

Hibernating helps animals to survive because they use so little energy. Their heartbeat and breathing slow down and their body chills. They can survive on nothing more than the fat they have stored in their body.

hedgehog

black bears

Did you know?

In some parts of the world, frogs, toads and tortoises sleep through the hottest season because food and water are difficult to find.

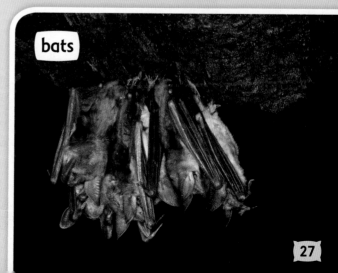
bats

Sleep Matters

Sleep is important for all animals and that includes humans, too. Now you know how much sleep matters, what changes might you make to your everyday life?

Keep out of your brother's way when he's tired and grumpy.

Stop using the computer before bedtime.

Be nice to your sister when she has had a bad dream.

Have a good night's sleep before a school test.

Try not to wake a baby when they're fast asleep.

Glossary

burrow: a hole dug by an animal for shelter

chemicals: substances that are in the body; our bodies need some chemicals to grow and be healthy

disease: an illness or sickness in the body

hibernation: a long, deep sleep in cold weather

nap: a short sleep

predators: animals that hunt other animals for food

roost: when birds or bats rest or go to sleep

Index

Look Back, Explorers

What is hibernation?

Where do flamingos sleep?

How many hours' sleep does someone aged seven need?

Look at pages 6 and 7. Can you explain what happens in the pattern of a normal day?

Page 17 tells us that 'artificial light can keep us awake'. Can you give some examples of artificial light?

Did you find out why bats sleep upside down?

Explorer Challenge: to help them take off when they need to fly (page 23)

What's Next, Explorers?

Now you know about the importance of sleep, go on a magic key adventure with Biff and Chip, when they visit a town where everyone seems to be asleep ...

Wake Up!

Series created by Roderick Hunt and Alex Brychta

OXFORD

Explorer Challenge
for *Wake Up!*

Find out who wears this nightcap ...